Shine Baby!

Find your spark, light up your world!

Melinda Watts

with Dianna Hobbs

Introduction

Arise, shine, for your light has come,
and the glory of the LORD rises
upon you.

Isaiah 60:1 NIV

Be your best. You're my princess.

Introduction

Growing up in Bridgeton, New Jersey, those are the words my awesome mom, Mary Pickett, always whispered in my ear to motivate me to give my all. Each time, her soft encouraging pep talk worked like a bright, shiny, magic charm, to the point where I thought I was *actually* a princess back then… like really. I could have walked around with a blingy tiara on my head and a poofy tutu, and I would have felt completely comfortable with that.

"Your Royal Highness," my dad, Franklin Pickett, confirmed from an early age that I was very special to him. He told me his "royal" little girl was supposed to wear only pink and sparkles. And I believed him too! Yep, those were the good old days. I was wide-eyed and innocent, creative, ambitious, and a free spirit. With a loving and supportive family motivating me, inspiring me to follow my passions, and creating a safe environment for me to dream big, I was confident I could soar way high up in the clouds.

Although I wasn't quite sure of the path my life would take, I knew I loved to sing. In fact, I had a blast pretending I was the late Whitney Houston and letting my hairbrush *have it*! When I closed my eyes, I envisioned a crowd of people listening and then bursting into applause. "Thank you so much!" I said to my imaginary audience. It's pretty obvious that I had an active imagination back then. I was also very sure of what I wanted to do from the time I was six years old. I was going to be a singer, but not just any kind.

I was focused on being a Gospel singer and touching people's hearts with God's love. Many days, I was at home making up melodies in my head— some good, others, pretty embarrassing. Thank God there was no YouTube then; otherwise, there would be hundreds of seriously humiliating videos of me circulating on the Internet!

While I was having a good time singing whatever popped into my head, I didn't know God was developing the songwriter in me. I was simply following my passions and boy did I have *a lot* of those. Aside from music, I got a kick out of simple things like wearing weird clothes and creating funky little outfits for my friends. I have always loved fashion and still do. I guess I was a big ball of creativity with no fears about expressing myself and celebrating all the things that made me uniquely Melinda.

But things began changing in my early teen years as I struggled to find myself in a suburban high school. My free-spiritedness was replaced by insecurity. I remember searching for other girls who looked similar to me and that I could identify with on different levels. When that didn't pan out, I even tried to piece together an identity from what I saw on TV and on the pages of magazines. That only made things worse. The famous models, Hollywood actresses and popular starlets didn't have hair, skin, or a body type like mine.

Unlike these days when thick legs and a thick curves are accepted as attractive traits, as a teen, my shape and ethnic features were not celebrated. So I questioned my value and doubted my personal beauty because of what I was around. My imaginary childhood tiara lost its glow with age and I wasn't feeling particularly special anymore. I lost that spark in my eyes that made me proud to be unique.

Still, I knew how to make friends, pretend I was happy and go along as if everything were okay. Deep down, though, I was really sad, hurting and feeling like an outcast. Beneath my big smile and cheerful attitude, I didn't believe I was cool or in any way part of the in-crowd. I secretly saw myself as an outsider wanting so badly to fit in. Low self-esteem robbed daddy's sparkling, pretty princess of her inward glimmer. The clock had struck twelve.

My coach turned into a pumpkin. And there was no Fairy Godmother to wave a magic wand to make my weight and skin problems disappear.

Just like that, I felt stuck in an emotional rut like hundreds of young girls and teens across the U.S. who attend my *Dream Girlz Gathering GLAM Camp* conferences.

The burden of low self-esteem was heavy upon me while I was developing into a woman because I didn't know how to completely like or accept myself. I cannot count how many times I have seen my former self reflected in the cheerless eyes of sweet, gifted and wonderful girls I help mentor. That's the beauty of life. You can experience things that will help someone else later on in life. The most important thing is to learn from them.

If I had known then what I know now I would have held tightly to the truth of Psalm 139:14 that says I am "fearfully and wonderfully made" in the image of an amazing God. That means I am hand-crafted by the same almighty God who created heaven and earth. He made me special! I didn't see it then, but I do today. Now I want others to believe and recognize the same thing about themselves.

I want you to know that You! Yes you! You rock! You're one of a kind. You are royalty. You have a spark within you that can light up the whole world. Your unique spark can be the game changer in someone else's life. That's why it's important to find it, cultivate and let it SHINE BABY!

The Bible even says so in 1 Peter 2:9. It calls you a "chosen people, a royal priesthood, a holy nation, a people belonging to God." Feeling special yet? Good! I want you to. I wrote this book specifically for you, to help you recognize that you are a jewel that is designed to shine for the glory of God.

You see, jewels or gems come in a variety of colors and shapes, but they are *all* beautiful treasures found in the deepest parts of the earth. Each gem is unique, rare, and oh so precious, just like the one holding this book in her hands. Yes, you! You are a priceless, brilliant jewel, made *to shine baby*.

I know you might not feel that way all the time and yet, it's true.

Although you may be wrestling with negative thoughts that tell you, you are not good enough, smart enough, pretty enough, or gifted enough to shine, don't believe the lies. With God on your side and the powerful keys I will share in this book that have helped *me* along the way, you can bury the burden of insecurity and uncover the hidden gem in you.

If I, by the grace of God, have been able to be a shining example for Christ, you can do the same thing! It won't always be easy to dig through all the negative thoughts and uncover that brilliant spark inside, but when it gets hard Philippians 4:13 says, you can do all things through Christ who gives you strength.

Through Jesus Christ you can be the bold, confident, glimmering jewel He designed you to be, at any age. No matter who you are or where you're from, God has a plan for your life. Even today, He is preparing you for your divine purpose, though you may not even know it.

I can truly say I had no idea when I started seriously writing songs when I was just fifteen years old (These melodies were a big improvement from the ones I created when I was six, thank the Lord!), that God was preparing me for a professional music career down the road. Sure, I wanted to be a singer, but the dream seemed so big and unlikely. I had no way of knowing that a local girl originally from New Jersey would be signed to a record deal. I didn't foresee releasing my very first album called *People Get Ready* featuring some of my own songs I had written. I couldn't have known my new CD would open up opportunities for me to travel around the country ministering to so many different people. If you had told me all that beforehand, I would have said, *no way!* I would have LOL'd big time.

My Story

All those things I just mentioned came about in a *totally* unconventional way that I'll share in a minute. But, before I talk about the amazing life-changing journey God took me on after winning Gospel Music Channel's *Gospel Dream* national talent search series, I so have to take you back to my first big break onto the national scene—something that set the stage for God's greater plan!

I was 18 years old when I got the chance to compete in a talent competition held on BET's hit inspirational talk show, Teen Summit. Being on one of the top-rated shows on television was a *huge* deal at the time. And there I was, singing my Gospel song and giving all I had in front of super famous judges like Jermaine Dupri, Teddy Riley, and others in their heyday.

Whew! Talk about intimidating. I was shaking in my boots like an earthquake hit me. But the Lord was with me as well as my family, friends, and mentors. I ended up being chosen as first runner-up out of all the extremely talented contestants from across America. Although a rapper walked away with the first place prize from Teen Summit, that experience built my confidence and was a major self-esteem booster. It helped me see that if I trusted

God enough to reach for the stars, the gift of singing He gave me would someday uplift and inspire all kinds of people. That exciting moment was simply a preview of my real breakthrough.

The year was 2008 when that "greater plan" I mentioned a moment ago was finally revealed. By then, my teenage years were long gone. My national BET debut was a distant memory. More than 10 years had passed. I was now a wife, mom, high school teacher and mentor to teen girls. I was pouring my heart and soul into a foundation I started, called *Project Sunday,* where I offered mentorship and help to young women in my community. On top of that, I had also set up *Heaven's House for Girls* to help out troubled teens and their families. I was one busy bee! Although I still absolutely loved singing and was actively creating new melodies, my priorities had changed.

I was a worship leader at my church and serving God with my gift, but had no immediate plans to pursue my music career. My plate was full and I was sort of content for the time being, you know? I had decided to settle into my wife and mommy role and put my musical dreams on hold... at least for a while.

Aside from having my hands full, somewhere along the way, my big ginormous dreams, though they were still within me, seemed almost *too big* to achieve. That free-spirited six-year-old no longer lived in me. My hairbrush was no longer a part-time imaginary microphone. The Whitney wannabe had been replaced by a woman who locked her giant-sized dreams in a tiny box labeled "someday" and threw away the key. But the time had come to let go of my fears and release my vision from inside that box. I just didn't know it yet.

When the opportunity to audition for Gospel Music Channel's Gospel Dream talent search presented itself, I was at home on maternity leave, taking a break from work. My husband William and I were so excited to be parents to our two month old baby, Lyric. I wanted to stay home with her for a while, because the fact that we even had a daughter was almost unreal. You see, doctors had told me I could never have children, so our baby girl was our miracle from God. When I got the shocking news that I was pregnant, we were like O-M-G! William and I were overjoyed. Lyric was the best surprise ever.

And when our sweet princess finally made her entrance into the world, we were in awe.

That's why it took some serious convincing to get me to try out for the Gospel Dream talent search. My newborn was my whole world. Had my sister Kisha not been *so good* at talking me into it (She can convince almost anyone to do anything.), I don't think I would have seriously considered competing.

At first, even with her inspiration, I wasn't so sure. But then, one day, I was sitting at home nursing, when it hit me. If I wanted to inspire other girls, like the ones I mentored through Project Sunday, to go after *their* dreams, I had to lead by example.

I even thought about tiny little Lyric, who would one day grow into a woman. I realized I needed to take action if I expected her to be able say, "Mommy followed her purpose and I can too!" It was a true *aha* moment.

Still, I was concerned about how I would balance my role as a new mommy with the pursuit of my music career. That just seemed way too hard in my mind. Knowing I would be separated from Lyric for a period of time was almost too much to bear. Kissing and holding her tiny little body, watching her sleep, and pouring all my love on her, was all I wanted to be doing.

Feeling unsure, I asked God for guidance. I needed to know, like yesterday, *"How in the world would this all work out?"* It would be nice if I could tell you I had my answer before I tried out for Gospel Dream, but nope. I didn't. As you live, learn and grow, you'll find out that no one ever knows how everything will turn out when it comes to embracing their big shine baby moment. You either go for it or you don't. I went for it.

When I seized that moment, everything in my life changed so fast it was dizzying, like a rapidly spinning ride at an amusement park. After I was chosen to be featured on the show, I continued advancing to higher levels of the competition. It was like *whoa*! Everything was exciting and scary all at once. I was under so much pressure to perform well despite everything else I had going on inside my head. That made it tough to enjoy the process at times. On the outside, I was happy and grateful for the amazing things that were going on in my life. But, on the inside, not knowing what the future held for me, made me really anxious.

No one knew how much I was struggling like God did, along with my my family and close friends. William was my rock and was always super comforting during a time where I was joyful and sad at the same time. When I was an emotional mess I could go to him for support, motivation and the love I needed. Looking back on it now, without a great support system, I would have never ever made it through that!

I remember I used to call my sister Kisha up before filming episodes. I would go on and on about my worries. I was a total train wreck some days. I missed Lyric. I didn't know where all this was leading. My family was making sacrifices for this dream. I was nervous about performing. I wasn't sure I was doing the right thing. The list went on and on. There were swarms of thoughts crowding my brain, increasing my worry and anxiety. I thought I would break down, but God held me up.

Once I shook off those natural jitters, I pulled myself together with prayer. I rehearsed all the uplifting things loved ones told me. I got out there on that stage, blocked everything out, gave it my best try, and leaned on God every step of the way. As I was singing, although the idea of winning the competition was a thrilling thought, it wasn't my primary focus. I was too busy praying and asking God for grace to pursue music, and be an amazing mommy I wanted to know how *that* was going to work!

I wasn't 100% sure it could... not even 50% sure. I had some serious internal and physical stuff going on. On the final day of taping the show, I discovered that going so long without nursing my precious newborn had caused my body to stop producing milk for her. I was so hurt that I wouldn't be able to give baby Lyric any more of Mommy's natural breast milk. Ugh!

"Tis so sweet to trust..." Right? That was the name of the hymn I sang on the last episode of Gospel Dream and I was *so* gone. At that point, I had nothing to lose. Inside, I understood that my life would change—win or lose. It already had, in fact. So my husband and I banded together with one focus: God and God only. I sang with everything I had as if I were in church, not on a nationally televised singing competition. I just shut everything out. I was no longer fixated on the fact that there were three judges listening that I deeply respect: Martha Munizzi, J. Moss, and Big Jim Wright.

I laid it all out right there on the stage. After I sung, I cried and literally danced before the Lord. I didn't care what anyone thought about me. I couldn't even *hear* the judges at first because I heard God's voice whisper to me, "You're in the palm of my hand." From that point onward I knew God had me. When time came to reveal the final results of the show, after a few tense moments spent holding hands with the other two amazingly gifted contestants, I heard the host call out *"Melinda Watts!"*

I could have fainted right on national TV! But instead, I just covered my face and cried so, so hard. "Wow! God, *really?*" I was thinking, because the other two finalists were crazy talented. I remember wiping away tears and looking for William. Then, there was that ache in my heart again. I started missing Lyric. I wanted to hold, rock and kiss my beautiful bundle of joy. My face was being seen across America, but my heart was at home with my baby. I'm mommy first, so my "gospel dream" has always been firmly anchored in reality.

Briefly, that same nagging question popped right back up. *"How will this all work?"* I wanted to know, but I would have to wait and see. In the meantime, I relaxed and celebrated the win. It was my shine baby moment and there have been many more for me since that time, just as there are many more for you.

A shine baby moment has nothing to do with selfish ambition and desiring to be in the spotlight to win approval. It has everything to do with taking center stage—whatever size the platform may be— to reflect the light of Christ for the world to see. When you agree to shine, you embrace your purpose, push past your trepidation and become the kind of vessel God can use for His glory.

If you will commit to reading every page in this book, you will find wisdom, personal stories—both mine as well as those of a few of my friends—that will help you discover the hidden spark in you.

If there is one thing I want you to carry away from this book, it is the knowledge that you are a priceless treasure, created and chosen by God to be an example of His greatness. God has a spark in you that can light up the world! There's only one you and the world is waiting for you to ignite!

Now turn the page and let me begin to show you how.

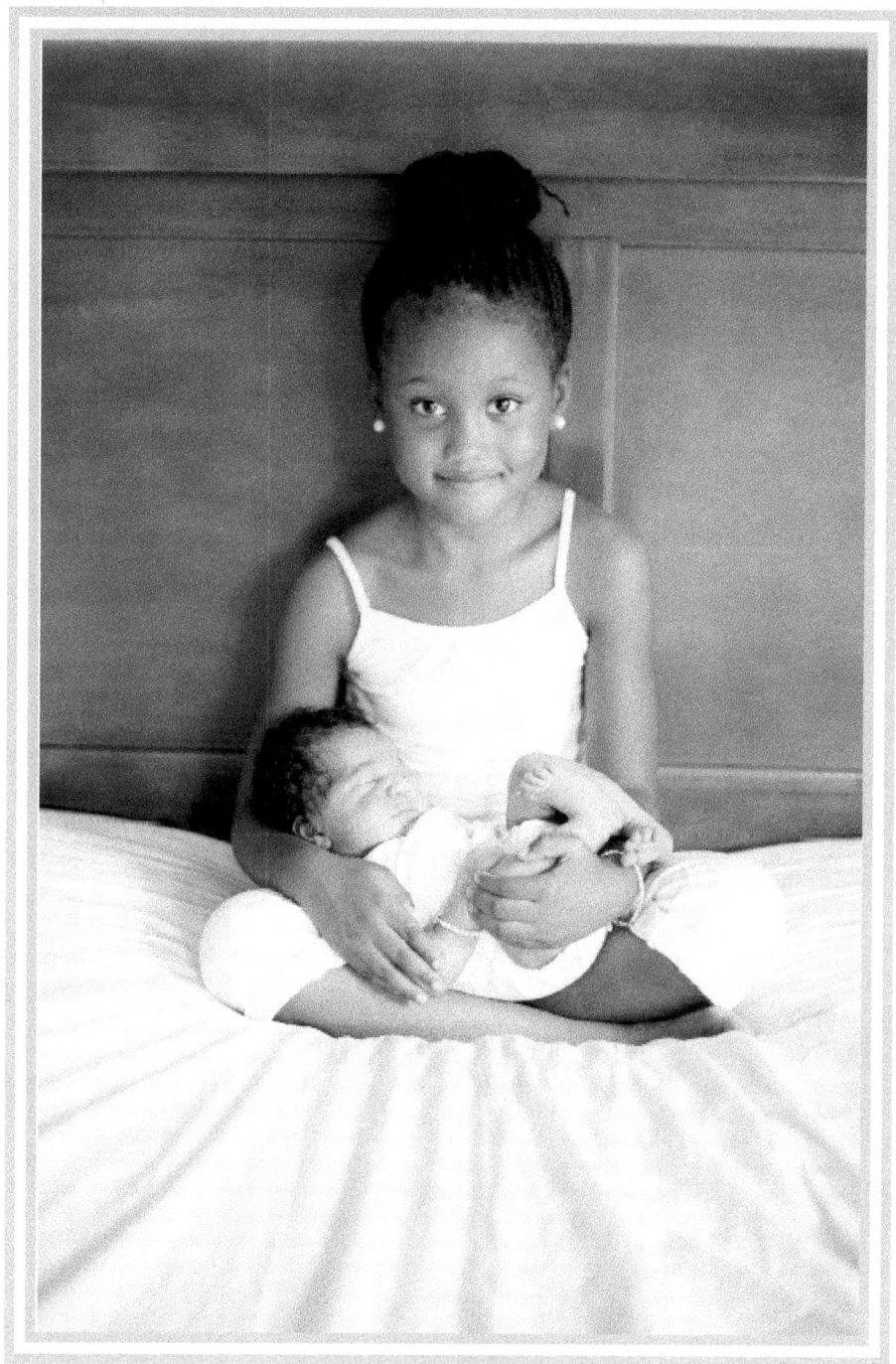

God places passions inside
each of our hearts to shine
light on the path that leads to
our destiny.

Passion

Passion

Right after I won Gospel Music Channel's Gospel Dream talent search, I was invited to headline a major musical event in Chattanooga, Tennessee by a ministry group that had seen the program. It was my very first "professional" engagement and honestly, I didn't know what to expect. But happily, I accepted the invitation. I felt nervous, honored and humbled that someone would graciously extend a platform for me, a total newbie, to minister in song. As someone fresh on the music block, all the business of handling a music career seemed so overwhelming, but in a wonderful and exciting way.

Sadly, the emotional rush I felt came to a screeching halt shortly after I arrived in Chattanooga on an October evening. The agreed upon arrangements were not honored and I was treated very poorly. Though the lack of hospitality was a big uncomfortable shock to my system, I had come to glorify God with my gift and that's just what I was determined to do.

Knowing I was last on the program, which is typical for the headliner, I patiently awaited my turn... and waited... and waited. It felt like ions went by! The event was so long, that by the time I took the stage, almost everybody had left. There were only around 12 people remaining. Yes, you read that right. The attendees had gotten irritated and restless, and didn't stick around for the conclusion of the matter. I was disheartened.

I looked out into a darkened, mostly empty auditorium, from a stage full of bright lights. There I stood all dolled up, watching a steady stream of people file out the door like an army of ants marching toward sugar. It depressed me. I was so troubled in my spirit even while singing, *"Have Thine Own Way Lord."* But I still had to minister through my disappointment.

I heard the Lord speak to me in a clear voice, causing me to stop mid-melody. He told me if I humbled myself despite the way people treated me, without allowing the actions of others to negatively impact what I do for Him, He would use me. More specifically, God gave me a timeframe for the manifestation that would take place in my music ministry: one year from that date. Though I wasn't sure what the Lord was planning to do in my life, I trusted His word.

I knew He was speaking to my heart when He challenged me to sing the way I would if there were 20,000 people in the audience. Those were His *exact* words. Though it was difficult (There weren't even 20 people left!), I obeyed God. In that very moment, I began seeing thousands of people in the spirit, even though there were only a handful of actual people present. I was having a vision of something that hadn't happened yet, which was enough to motivate me to keep going. Overcome by God's presence, I paused and said, "Thank you to whoever invited me. If you could only see what I see…"

I don't know if they thought I was nuts or not, but I stood there with my head held high. I was crying on the inside, yet, I still had supernatural peace. The taste of reality that night was bitter, but the word God inspired me to expect better, greater and more in the future. Giving my life over to the pursuit of music ministry didn't look so attractive right then and there. It wasn't exactly the ideal way to kick off a lifelong career! Nevertheless, in the midst of it all, the Holy Spirit continued to fuel my passion.

I'm not saying hearing a word from the Lord suddenly made things easy.

If I told you that, I would be telling a lie, because things actually got worse that night. After I finished ministering, I had to find my own way back to the hotel in this strange place. No one made any arrangements for my ground transportation. Yikes! To top it all off, those who invited me didn't say a word—not thank you, goodbye, or boo. Once again, God assured me that if I decided that none of those exterior circumstances mattered as much as me releasing what I was supposed to give that night, He would get glory through me. And you know what? God kept His promise to me.

Exactly one year later, I was singing at Bishop T.D. Jakes' *Woman Thou Art Loosed* conference, astounded by God's faithfulness and favor. When I got back to my seat after ministering in front of a jam-packed audience of thousands, I wept with a heart full of thanksgiving. The multitude of people I had seen in the *spirit* while standing before an audience of 12 in Chattanooga, were there in the *flesh* that night as I sang *"Faith."*

God is amazing, isn't he? The two experiences were night and day. There was one thing, however, that remained the same. Although the audience size was different, my passion and desire to please the Lord was as strong as it was a year prior. It still wasn't about numbers, amenities, or anything else. It was about my love for ministry. This is what led me to seize and maximize that shine baby moment for God!

Don't Let Anyone Steal Your Passion

I love the song *"Can't Give Up Now"* by Mary Mary. The words speak of keeping the faith even when you get tired along the way, because, sometimes, you will get downright exhausted. Trust me, I know. There have been *many* seasons in my life when I've considered giving up on everything. I have wanted to quit plenty of times.

There have been nights when I've cried myself to sleep; days when disappointments and failures momentarily crushed my spirit; and situations when relationships fell apart after people I trusted, intentionally deceived me. And yet, God has used the power of passion to keep me moving ahead in my weakest moments.

I believe that passion is that invisible driving force that makes you try again and again, even when you feel alone, afraid and apprehensive about the future. Passion, despite the trials that arise in pursuit of it, gets in your spirit and invades your thoughts. You wake up and go to sleep thinking about that thing that has a firm grip on the deepest desires of your heart.

Gospel music was that thing for me, even though that dream was almost lost at thirteen years old. Had it not been a true passion of mine, I would not have recovered when a leader I deeply respected said something hurtful and damaging to me. "You'll never make it in music because you aren't black enough and your voice doesn't squall enough," they said. I was in shock! I completely trusted this person's opinion. So when I was told my style was too different to be embraced by different audiences, I was messed up about it. I had always liked different styles of music. What was wrong with that?

I balled my eyes out at home. I didn't know how to feel other than broken. Sure, I was unique. I loved all kinds of music and had been influenced by everything from Country to Arabian. I loved to worship the Lord and Traditional Gospel simply wasn't the only thing in my cup of tea. But still, did that person have to say *that?* Here I was, an insecure teen, devastated by the unfeeling words of a trusted mentor. Just like that, this person almost stomped out my long-held and longshot dream of becoming a singer.

What many people don't know about me is that I do not come from a musical family. Neither of my parents sings. Can you believe that? My father is a chef. My mom is a teacher and counselor, and my sister Kisha is a nurse (She's great at nursing, too, but I wanted nothing to do with that!). Me? Well, singing has always been my thing. As far back as I can remember I loved to hear the sound of my own voice belting out notes.

My dad, my personal male cheerleader, recognized my gift. He made me practice every day after school, which helped me greatly improve. It took a lot of dedication too. In addition to my rehearsals, my grandmother, Sarah, used to always play quartet music. Those sort of melodies with a down home country feel were her favorites! Pastor Shirley Caesar was blasting around the house all the time and I loved her. I was gaga over music and was glued to the radio each and every time I came over Grandma Sarah's house for a visit.

God was planting seeds in my heart and connecting me to music, my future career. Over time, I got serious about it. I asked to move my bedroom into my parents' basement to give me a personal space to create music—a pretty unusual request for a thirteen-year-old! I probably was tripping a little bit, but my always-supportive parents consented. I had my own downstairs pad where I sang as much as I wanted to. It was the coolest thing! At least it was for me.

But my poor unsuspecting parents had no idea what they had agreed to. They probably would have said no if they knew their little girl would sing so loudly that they would be forced to close all the doors to muffle my strong voice. Many days, my mother would beg me to quiet down. But I found it hard to comply because I was constantly practicing. Eventually, they got used to my singing sessions, closed the doors behind me, and just let me do my thing. The more I sang, the more I believed in myself. That's why I was heartbroken when my mentor told me there was no way I could do the very thing I worked so hard to perfect.

I just remember, in the midst of my tears, crying out to God in prayer and hearing His voice in my distress that day. That's why I know He speaks to young people for sure. He said to me, "I can hear your heart even if your mouth is glued shut. It's not what comes out of your mouth but what's in your heart that I hear. Do what's in your heart." That was a life-changing word from God that helped me a lot.

Of course that wasn't the end of the opposition I would face in my life, nor was it the last time I would feel hurt over not-so-nice comments from others. I learned from it, however, that God's presence is the perfect antidote for wounded hearts. He helped me learn to say, "Hey, I'm different from others and that's okay, but I'm still chosen by God!" I'm living proof that when your passion is fueled by the presence of God, you are then able to move beyond tears and into purpose. What others think of you, say and do to you, won't matter as much.

Mix Your Passion With Prayer

Ask anyone who is living out their divine calling day-to-day and they'll tell you, before they got started, their passion gave them a huge clue about what their purpose would be. God places desires for certain things inside each of our hearts to shine light on the path that leads to our destiny. But it is not only our inner yearning that gives our lives direction. We also have to pray and seek the Lord about exactly what our divine assignment is and how we should use our gifts and talents to that end.

That's why I say passion should always be mixed with prayer. Otherwise, our pursuits will be self-directed rather than God-ordained, which is a true recipe for disaster. We have to remember every *good* thing is not a *God* thing and everything *we* want is not necessarily what *God* wants for us.

Personally, I have to constantly stay in prayer so the Holy Spirit drives my passion and not my flesh. If I don't seek the Lord, I'll be all over the place, because naturally, I'm outgoing and goals-driven. I like to try out new things. I have multiple interests and ideas competing for my attention on any given day. If it was left up to me, I probably would try to do far too many things. I would likely end up off course, frustrated and exhausted, because I love helping everybody.

During my school years, I was a part of groups like: Student Leadership, Safety Patrol, Girl Scouts and more, because they allowed me to serve. I felt fulfilled when pouring into others, so I did lots of that! For some reason, I was seriously bothered anytime I saw schoolmates suffering at home. I wanted to do anything I could to make things better. My passion for helping would just overtake me. Before I knew it, I would spring into action to save the day.

I knew everyone wasn't raised in a happy home like me. My hard-working parents were still married. They did all they could to provide a stable life for me and my sister. We were loved, nurtured, well cared for and content. We were also encouraged to excel in school and were rewarded handsomely when we did. Whenever I received good grades, I could get whatever I wanted from my dad, so I made sure to perform well academically. I was very blessed indeed.

However, some of my friends at school weren't so fortunate. Although I couldn't change their situation, I did what I could, which was to encourage them. I would tell them all the things I learned in church, hoping something would uplift their hearts. I felt like Peter in Acts 3:6 when he said, "Silver or gold I do not have, but what I have I give you…" Anything I could share that would make their going a little easier, I would do it in a heartbeat.

Giving was and is my passion. It made me feel great! It has definitely carried over into adulthood too. The only difference now is, through prayer, God has revealed ways for me to channel, discipline and structure that passion so I don't wear myself out. When I look at my life these days, although I fill multiple roles, they all work together to fulfill my divine assignment. Only God could bring that kind of order to my life and yours. I know I am not that organized! I commit my life to him through prayer. Then, our

Heavenly Father takes all the pieces of the puzzle and puts them together. Try it. It truly works.

When it comes to all the wonderful things you have inside you to give, you need to balance that. The only way you can do that is through seeking God for His help. He'll show you what you should be doing, as well as when, where and how. But God won't barge into your life and begin taking over things just because He's able to do anything. You have to invite Him in to rule over your life.

Be Passionate And Realistic

As much as I appreciate wonderful musical compositions, I am not a music producer. And since I know I'm not a producer or musician, I don't try to be one. Instead, I bring my lyrics and melodies to someone who knows how to put together beats and instruments to complement the song. Without a producer, my songs would sound a hot, disorganized mess! There would be no completed composition. Knowing this helps me stay in my lane: singing, creating lyrics and catchy melodies. This practical way of thinking keeps me from pursuing a life course that doesn't fit with my gifts and talents. It also helps me avoid wasting energy on things I don't have the knowledge, skill, or ability to take on.

Being passionate without being realistic is dangerous! It leads you on a reckless path to disappointment. That's why being prayerful about your passion and purpose is important. It invites God in to show you what He really called you to do. Here's a tip for you. If there is no anointing and gifting associated with your desires, they do not represent a truly divine passion. God never calls you without equipping you, nor does He equip you without leading you.

He knows that before we are able to shine for Him, we need Him to first shine *His light* on the path we must travel to our destiny. He literally shows us which way to go and God never runs out of ways to confirm our purpose.

One day, I walked into the grocery store and began humming a tune in the produce section. I got so carried away. I must have thought I was in the space my parents set aside for me in their basement years ago. I honestly didn't realize others could actually hear me. To my surprise, a woman who was small in stature walked up to me and said "I love your voice. You should record it so everyone can hear it." Her words made me view my gift in a whole new way and a light bulb went off in my head. I thought, "Why not record? If she wants to hear it, maybe others will too! "

After we have prayed and sought God about His will for our lives, He will use something as simple as a grocery store conversation to turn our attention toward our God-given dreams that are yet unrealized. Someone may encourage us to take a closer look at a talent we've been taking for granted.

God may allow us to be asked to exercise a gift we didn't know we had. As a result, we amaze ourselves when we do an extraordinary job. The Lord could even place it on someone's heart to invest in our calling in order to get us to the next level. He already knows the plans He has for us. And when our spiritual passions are in the right place, God will help us get all our practical matters in place. Things will begin lining up.

All it takes is mixing your passion with prayer and acting on whatever God places in your heart to do. Don't be afraid. After all, He didn't give you those desires and dreams just to sit on them. You were created to shine for His glory. Those gifts inside you were made to be shared with the world, so begin putting them to use. Don't worry about obstacles, criticisms, or limitations. The power of your divinely inspired passion is stronger than anything that comes to hinder you!

Spark of Wisdom for Letting Your Passion Shine:

Delight yourself in the LORD and he will give you the desires of your heart.

~Psalm 37: 4 NIV

The most important passion you will ever have is a passion to please God. Every other passion should come from this primary one. So delight in the Lord. Meditate on His word. And make sure your spiritual walk is right. When you do, the God who loves and cares about you so much will implant His passion into your heart and you will see manifestation. Then, as your desires line up with His will for your life, things will fall into place.

Shine Baby!

Personality

Even though we are imperfect,
our God-given personality is
perfect for fulfilling our purpose

Personality

Do you ever see those people who appear to have it all together, like they are totally in control? It's seems like they never have an off day and a hair is never out of place. That's an exaggeration, but you know what I mean. They just look strong, confident and able to do almost anything with no sweat—the total opposite of you. It's easy to believe you would be better able to fulfill your life's purpose if you had a personality more like theirs. But that is not true! Flaws and all, God can and will use you to shine for Him.

As the saying goes, the grass always looks greener on the other side. But if you take a stroll over there to take a closer peek, you'll recognize that it's no different than what is growing in your own front lawn. In other words, the qualities and talents you already possess are just as good as what the next person has. You just need nurturing to be the best you can be. That's it! In this chapter, we will explore how God can use you with all your unique characteristics to do great things.

Whether you are bold and feisty; shy and reserved; high-strung and outgoing; or cool, calm and collected, you will see that your personality is perfect for your purpose. That doesn't mean *you're* perfect. Hey, no one is. But the good news for you is that God will make up for what you lack. He'll also help you balance any extremes in your personality, as long as you seek Him for wisdom.

Sometimes you may struggle and feel like you are not the right one for the job because of "the way you are." We all feel like that from time-to-time. But God created you that way and loves you as you are.

What if there are things in your life that aren't right? Glad you asked.

Any areas that need perfecting in you, as you submit to Him, God will take care of those by giving you supernatural power through His Holy Spirit to overcome. With Him, all things are possible! So don't think you can't fulfill your destiny because you can and you will uncover the hidden gems inside waiting to be revealed.

Sure, you might be a little rough around the edges right now. But God, who adores you, will work on you and make you better when you let Him in. He will even bring the right people and opportunities along to help you.

Before long, you'll begin seeing that you are somebody special, made in the image of God and created to shine. You are no different from the ordinary people you view as extraordinary. You, too, are sensational!

Don't be fooled by what you think you see in others' personalities and assume they have, know and can do so much more than you. I used to believe that same lie once upon a time. But if it were true, God could not have pulled me out of the background with all my limitations. Although I am painfully shy and often feel uncomfortable when it comes to being out front—Really, I do!— God helps me overcome this personality quirk. With His strength, I am able to dig deep down and discover the bold, outgoing, tenacious part of me.

Through my experiences, I'm about to reveal how you can begin to better understand, embrace and handle your personality. That way, it won't stop your progress or keep you from sparkling like the beautiful jewel you are.

Purpose is Stronger Than Personality

I remember when I was just a pigtail-wearing nine-year-old singing in the youth choir every fourth Sunday. I had such a blast churning out melodies with my friends from church. But it never occurred to me that God wanted to draw me out from the crowd and put my vocal gift on display—at least not until Christmas season rolled around one year.

For some reason, no one wanted to sing the popular Christmas carol, *Silent Night*. I mean, like, everyone knows that song. So why didn't anyone want to sing it? Beats me, but they all backed out, creating an urgent need for a fill-in. I knew in my heart I could sing that beautiful melody. I just knew *it*! But I was way too afraid to throw my hat into the ring. I was small and inexperienced and had not sung openly since my preschool graduation. Our director, Lester Taylor was looking for lead singers and even though I was small I wanted a shot!

Although a part of "Princess Melinda" was confident, outgoing and determined, I lacked a little bit in the courage department when it came to campaigning for the spotlight. But my never-take-no-for-an-answer childhood bestie Regina made sure I seized upon that opportunity. Regina never let me back out of a challenge. She's the reason why I was a dare devil in many ways growing up. All my bathroom solos she witnessed were enough to convince her that

I needed to be heard right away. So she made it her personal mission to see to it that I was the chosen one for the Christmas solo. Gulp!

I just stood back and watched as my self-appointed spokesperson, without a trace of fear, walked right up to the preacher and said, "Make her sing. She can sing. Make her sing!" Even though the Minister of Music told Regina I was too little, that didn't stop her from pressing the issue. In the end, her go-getter attitude more than made up for my shy personality. She pushed forward while I shrank backward, hiding in the shadows. I couldn't believe what she was attempting to do, but you know what? It worked! She paved the way for my big holiday singing debut. And oh what a glorious day it was.

If I could turn back the hands of time so you could personally witness that moment, I would do it. You would agree that my purpose, even then, was way stronger than my bashful personality. When I held the microphone up to my mouth, something overtook me. Fear melted away. All that sheepishness that held me back seemed to disappear. I closed my eyes, made that song my own and poured my heart into it. I was so serious about singing that carol that the whole choir was stunned silent! It really was a silent night. When it was all over, my first church solo went so well, I was the designated person to lead that carol at Christmas time for the next six years. My Pastor, Pastor Morgan put me behind the pulpit every year and that was something that I looked forward to. He saw something in me from a child and he helped develop that gift. I am so thankful to him for that.

Looking back on it, I can see God's hand was all over my life. The Lord knew all those years ago He wanted to use me, a timid little girl, to sing for Him. He also knew I couldn't bless masses of people with my voice while hiding in the bathroom! Thank God for Regina or I might still be singing into my brush pretending to be on stage. Even if I would have eventually come across my shine baby moment without her help, it may have taken much longer to do so.

SPARK: What about your own life? Can remember a time when God used a person or opportunity to help you do what your personality made it hard to accomplish? They might have stood up for you; given you access to resources, people and things you needed to succeed; or shared information that made it much easier to do well in a certain area. If you think long and hard, you'll probably come up with all sorts of great memories of helpers who have touched your life in some way. Hopefully this book will become one of those helpers for you.

As you recall those special people and opportunities, let the memories comfort you when you feel like your personality makes it hard to get ahead. Let their assistance in your life remind you that there is no need to worry. God has your back… and front… and side. He'll make up for what you lack in personality. As long as you trust Him and step up to the plate, your Heavenly Father will equip you to hit a homerun when your turn comes to bat.

Keep Your Personality In Check

There have been times in all of our lives when our personalities got the best of us and dimmed our bright light. If you are shy, you might say nervousness made you too jumpy to focus and do a good job. If you are courageous you might say, you got out there and tried something new before you were ready and made a mess. A person who is always relaxed and calm might say, they were in "chill mode" when they should have been working to get things done, resulting in a missed opportunity.

Maybe your personality struggle is just the opposite of shyness. Who knows? You might be boisterous, loud and too aggressive. If so, I can relate to that also. How? Well, my personality is a mixture. When it comes to standing up for me, I can be too laid back. But when my friends or family members are in trouble, I turn into a different person. I become bolder, stronger and braver. The protector comes out of me and fear goes right out the window.

It's like the one time in high school when my best friend NeNe got into it with a schoolmate. The girl who wanted to fight my bestie warned her about something terrible she intended to do. When I found out about what could possibly happen to NeNe, I got riled up. I don't play when it comes to NeNe so I was going to make things happen on my own. That's when my other, more outspoken side showed up on the scene. See, NeNe and I were so close that she was like a sister to me. I don't know why, but I felt personally responsible for her safety, even though she was very capable of fighting for herself. She could throw *down*!

NeNe, who was tough and cool, lived down the street from me and would hang out at my house all the time. The two of us, though very different, got along so well. We listened to music together, laughed, talked, made our favorite sausage sandwiches and enjoyed each other's company. Though my BFF was a lot hipper and I was considered more of the geeky type back in the day, NeNe never treated me like a square or thought I was corny.

She loved me for who I was, dorky and all. She cared for and embraced me the way any real friend should. I know it can be hard to find genuine people who don't judge you or shun you when you don't fit into their mold. So I valued our relationship and was not about to stand by and watch NeNe come into harm's way. It wasn't about to go down like that on my watch.

What I *should have* done was told an adult that my friend was being threatened with bodily harm. Why didn't I just speak up about what was going on and ask for help? That would have been the right way to handle it. But I took matters into my own hands, which ended in utter disaster. One of the worst mistakes of my life started with what seemed to be a perfect discovery. I thought I had found a way to defend my friend through watching one of my favorite TV shows called *MacGyver*. It was about the life of Secret Agent Angus MacGyver who could fix anything. He was some sort of super genius. The way this guy could solve complex problems using science and everyday items had me thinking I could do the same thing. I know it was ridiculous but it seemed to make logical sense at the time.

With my nerdy self, I came up with my own scientific idea for how to create an effective weapon for NeNe's protection. I actually heated up my homemade tool of defense on the stove to make it nice and sturdy. I told my dear friend not to worry about anything because, *dun dun dun*, "Super Melinda" would see to it that she was prepared for her fight.

I was out of my mind! I didn't realize how silly I looked and sounded, especially because I had never fought a day in my life. But I was so caught up in my emotions, I couldn't think straight. I let my bold personality take over and it got me into big trouble. I was way out of balance and had lost a complete grip on reality. I mean, I was getting tips from a fake TV character. Seriously, Melinda?

So anyway, I packed NeNe's specially prepared weapon and headed off to school all amped up. My best friend and I were on 10. We were so ready.

But let me be honest, I had no real plans to jump into the fight and come to blows. I had it all planned out. I would be like the ringside coach in a boxing match that helps their fighter win. I was working in an "advisory capacity" only. I just wanted to make sure NeNe, the experienced fighter, had what she needed to take care of this mean girl once and for all. That's really code for I was wimpy and scared.

But the two of us rocket scientists had not considered one very important detail before conjuring up this wild scheme. Um, there was a possibility that we might get caught at school with a weapon. Too bad we *didn't* take that into consideration… because it is precisely what happened. Needless to say, our big showdown turned out to be an epic fail, not exactly the ending we had imagined. Both NeNe and I came crashing down from our emotional high when we were expelled from school.

Boy did my daddy beat the brakes off me! My parents were so disappointed. They raised me to be a person of good character and judgment.

My dad always told me and my sister, "I want you to go further than I did." He wanted to see us make excellent choices and do well—nothing like the terrible stunt I had pulled. I was so ashamed of myself afterward.

I knew better, but I went all in and gave over to my feelings. I just reacted, which was a huge mistake that threatened to derail my education. Thank God I was able to get back on track and successfully graduate from high school and later, college. Still, that detour in my life didn't have to happen. I had heard my parents tell stories over and over again about how hard they worked to create a good life for me and my family. They were great providers and I was wasting time on foolishness by letting my "other personality" control me.

Growing up, my mom picked cotton in the field, just like the people I read about in my history books. She later drove the bus to earn a living. My father once worked in the onion field in Alabama and then headed off to Vietnam where he became a chef. He could do a mean thing in the kitchen too! During my years spent at home, I remember dad going to work at General Motors by night, while being a top chef by day. Clearly, my parents were hard workers and did their best to instill the value of diligence and education in us.

After NeNe and I landed in hot water, I cut out the antics and worked harder to redirect my personality and focus. I never did anything that dumb again, but instead, threw myself into my studies. Through that experience I learned, if you don't channel your personality and energy toward the right thing, you will be headed toward ruin and destruction. So keep your personality in check. When God begins to transform your heart, he gives you His identity. The more we seek after His heart, the more our personalities are shaped in a way that pleases Him. Even now I find myself asking God to continue to shape and mold me. That's something I find is challenging but also very rewarding.

Wisdom Is Greater Than Personality

As you see from the previous story, just because you have the courage to do something, doesn't mean you should. And just because you feel fear, doesn't mean you shouldn't do something. So how do you know what to do and when to do it? You need wisdom, which is the kind of knowledge and good judgment God gives us to handle situations properly.

Proverbs 4:7 says, "Getting wisdom is the wisest thing you can do! And whatever else you do, develop good judgment." The only way to get wisdom, which is even greater and more important than personality, is to ask God for it. James 1:5 says, "If you need wisdom, ask our generous God, and he will give it to you. He will not rebuke you for asking."

Wisdom helps you to stay in balance, avoid taking crazy risks and thrive in life with whatever characteristics you have. Good judgment will keep you from allowing your temperament or nature to completely control your actions. Without it, you will be at the mercy of your mood and emotions, which can be harmful if you're not in the right state of mind.

When you exercise wisdom, your natural tendencies, which could otherwise mess up good things in your life, will be kept in check. God will show you how to channel your feelings toward constructive things. He will teach you what thoughts, ideas, behaviors and environments are healthiest for someone of your nature, because He knows best. Although you cannot change the core of who you are, with wisdom as your foundation, you can position yourself to win in life. On the contrary, if you reject wisdom, you will make your journey so much harder than it has to be.

Take my daughter Lyric for example. She loves to build castles in the sand. Actually, she likes to build whatever she can think of in her mind that she believes will be amazing. My little diva is highly creative and independent like me. So, one day, while at the beach she said, "Mommy I'm going to build us a house in the sand so that we can live here on the beach forever!"

"Okay baby," I responded. "Let me know if you need my help with the bottom so it can stand up." Of course Lyric's strong-willed personality caused her to refuse my help. She prefers doing most everything on her own and the construction of a sandy beach house was *her* personal pet project. So I watched closely as Lyric tried and tried to gather the sand together to form block shapes. But nothing was working.

After several attempts, Lyric managed to mold the grains into a single tiny square, but it quickly crumbled and fell apart. And that, my friend, is what happens when we refuse wisdom, guidance and assistance. We end up working so hard to build something, only to have it all fall down like Humpty Dumpty. But why not ask for and receive the wise counsel of God, as well as other mature, trustworthy individuals He places in your life? What do you have to lose by being humble enough to let a more experienced person show you how to accomplish your goals faster and with greater ease? You have nothing to lose, but everything to gain by doing that. That's one of the biggest shine baby tips of all.

It is certainly how I have been blessed to prosper at so many things. All my life, I have drawn from the knowledge of those who have come before me. This balances out what my personality lacks. As I said earlier, wisdom is greater than personality. Even now, when I feel tempted to do stuff my own way, maturity tells me to be still, listen and abide by what I learn. There is always someone that knows something I don't know. And when there is not a physical person there to teach me, God guides me in other ways.

While doing an event for girls in Seattle, I met Latasha. My Lord was this girl smart! She was fun, funky, smart as a whip and an amazing photographer. As we grew our sisterhood, I learned so many things from her. I can't take a picture to save my soul, but she could take pictures with her eyes closed. More than that she could see a project that I wanted to work on in a different way. Like Oprah and Gayle, there was a balance of skill. One supported the other and things work! Don't try igniting the world with your spark all on your own. Your job is to find it and then allow God to connect you to others to use it!

If I tried to do all these things myself, I would have never gotten them done. Sometimes you need someone who knows more than you in a certain area to help you accomplish it! Sometimes You have to find your spark by letting someone else use their matches to light it. We all are on a journey together and other people will have the missing link to your puzzle along the way.

I don't know where I would be today without my God-mother Jackie. Seriously. She is one of the most amazing women that I know! She helps me work through so many things and helps push me into my purpose. My spark was ignited as a young girl in her hair salon. She saw the spark and committed to helping me find and cultivate it. I couldn't do that alone. Neither should you. God has people that He wants to strategically place in your life for purpose. His purpose!

Often, when I study the word of God, there are times when I will be reading the Bible or some other book that contains the answers I need. I may get inspired by an uplifting program I am watching on television that sparks an amazing idea. During my prayer and devotion time, God even speaks words directly to me that I need to hear. But being willing to listen is the key; that is the only way to get wisdom. I can't do this if I am being a know-it-all. Neither can you. Know-it-alls dismiss great advice because, well, they think they know it all! Usually, these same individuals end up frustrated with life and don't grow or succeed the way they could and should. Don't be one of those people, okay? Promise?

During my years as a California high school English teacher, I taught lots of kids who were considered disadvantaged and hard to reach. Some professionals had written them off as lost causes. But I knew they had great potential and didn't have to be defined by the unfair labels placed upon them.

I believed in these students and discovered that no matter how hard their lives were, they did great when they focused, paid attention and obeyed instructions.

Even with all the different personality types I dealt with on a daily basis, I saw that the teens most eager and willing to learn, regardless of their background, challenges, or temperament, excelled. When they opened their hearts and minds to receive new knowledge and benefit from the wisdom I shared from day to day, they triumphed.

That's why I encourage the young girls who come to the *Dream Girlz Gathering /GLAM Camp* conferences I host across America, to be lifelong learners. Listen to the positive adults who love and care about you. Parents, teachers, guidance counselors, church leaders, and other mentors—which we will discuss more in chapter 3—are there to help. The more you listen, the more you will know. The more you know, the more you will grow. And the more you grow, the higher you'll go!

One young woman named Mikaela Walsh who came to a Dream Girlz event wrote me an awesome letter about how much she learned from our time together. Her transformation shows the powerful wisdom and the benefits of having a deeper understanding of who God is. I want you to read part of Mikaela's letter below.

Before I came to the Gathering I already thought I had God in my heart and I was doing everything the right way. But I really was as far away as I could be. The moment I stepped into Dream Girlz Gathering I thought, "Well this is going to be boring and everyone is going to be into it and I'm not. I'm going to be the one that stands out." Then I met Melinda Watts and the minute I did, I knew she would help me find God and help me do what's right. And she did.

She showed me so many things I didn't even know. Things that I wouldn't do in public, I learned that it's okay to do those things because it's not about what other people think or say about you. It's all about you and God connecting together. The things Melinda and the Glam Girls talked about really touched me. During my time I saw other people and how they were touched the same way I was. Now I put my entire life in God's hands.

Wow! What an awesome testimony. Right? Being connected to God and experiencing His power, changes lives. Gaining wisdom of His greatness and inviting Jesus Christ into your heart sets your life on the right path. This is true for everyone, no matter your age, sex, race, ethnicity, background, or personality. The power of God is greater than all of it.

Spark of Wisdom for Letting Your Personality Shine:

In the same way, let your good deeds shine out for all to see, so that everyone will praise your heavenly Father

~Matthew 5:16

Your personality is given to you to assist you in doing the good work God has given you to accomplish. So when you make a choice to do a certain thing, ask yourself, *"Am I letting God shine through my personality or am I dimming the light of Christ through my bad behaviors and attitudes?"* If you are not sure what to do in a given situation, pray and ask God to show you the right way to go. You should always trust Him more than you trust yourself.

Shine Baby!

People

Every relationship is not right
for you, but the ones that are
will stand the test of time, and
help you shine all the more
brightly for Christ. Good relationships will light your spark and
keep you in your purpose.

People

As a rule, I don't hang out with negative people. I just don't allow people who always see the bad in everything into my circle. I'm way too giddy and optimistic to have Negative Nancy's rocking with me. Just doesn't fit well! So I do my best to surround myself with only positive friends and mentors who add good things to my life. In fact, those who are closest to me are the ones I want to be like in some way. That's because I know that people I spend most of my time with, will eventually rub off on me. And since I want to live a great life full of divine joy, peace and purpose, I keep company with the kind of folks who help and encourage me to stay on the right path. That makes sense, doesn't it?

If you want to be kind, compassionate and helpful, rolling with the mean, arrogant bullies obviously isn't the way to go. It's a good practice to look at your circle of friends. Pay attention to who is in your space and think about what kind of influence they are having over you. People who have the most of your time are the people who will impact how your life carries out. Of course everyone is not close enough to truly impact you, but you have to think about those relationships and their effect. Ask yourself " Are they going in my same direction? Are they supporting me and helping me? Am I a good fit for them?" All those questions will give you a good idea about where you are headed by the company that you keep.

Some people you only see in passing and basically keep the relationship on a "hi and bye" level. You might be "friends" on Facebook or follow each other on Twitter, but rarely talk in real life. You may even see each other at the mall or other events on occasion. These are just acquaintances. There is no genuine relationship there, so their involvement in your life is not that deep.

They have no real power and don't matter as much. On the other hand, when it comes to the ones you consider best friends and those you take advice from, you have to choose wisely. If you don't you could end up hurt and God doesn't want that to happen. He cares about the kind of people surrounding you, because they will either build you up or tear you down.

Choosing good relationships is so important, that I have devoted an entire chapter to helping you know how others fit (or don't fit) in your life. As you read carefully, also be praying about whether your clique or crew really clicks with you. To help you do that, I want to share an often used quote that says, "Show me your friends and I'll show you who you are."

So who are you? Who do you want to be? Do your friends reflect that? If not, it could be time to make some changes. As I stated before, you become like the people you hang around the most. If they are good, positive and wholesome, you are more likely to have those same qualities. However, if your inner-circle is full of trouble-makers that don't listen to anyone, you are setting yourself up for a bumpy ride through life.

When I was in college, I became really good friends with a guy who had his own choir. He was the kind of choir director that totally lived and breathed music. It was literally his life. Before we started hanging out, although I could sing, I didn't go to a lot of musicals and concerts, or run with those who did.

But tagging along with him exposed me to that lifestyle and created opportunities for me to sing. All of a sudden, my circle changed. His friends became my friends and it was an exciting time. Just like that, our relationship opened me up to a whole new world.

Before connecting with this dedicated choir director, I was just the new girl from "the country" who could sing. Once I started rolling with him, I conformed, blended and got heavily involved in music, just the way he did. I was becoming a different person, which thankfully, wasn't a bad thing at all in my case. But what if my guy friend had been into drinking, drugging, partying and wrong behaviors? By inviting him into my life and willingly sharing his interests, habits and social circles, I could have ended up on a very different path. Come to think of it, many of my high school and college peers got linked up with the wrong crowd and lost their identity.

Be careful not to make that mistake! It's easy to point the finger at those who run with the fast crowd, go buck wild and make embarrassing mistakes. But if you don't select your relationships carefully, you could also find yourself in the same situation. Only let positive, principled and purposeful people inside your circle; everybody else gets locked outside the gate with a huge "Keep Out" sign on it.

Know When To Let Go

Every once in a while, a close relationship you thought was healthy will go sour like "Lemonheads" candy after sweet yellow layer comes off. It's a real bummer when that happens, but it does. That person you once were so cool with may change for the worst or reveal that they never were who you thought they were from the beginning. It has happened to me before. I lost a close friend in college and I was so hurt. I wanted to hang on because I grew to love her and I enjoyed hanging out with her. Unfortunately, we grew apart and had different interests. There will be a time when you have to let go. When it becomes necessary, like it or not, you have to walk away.

I have seen bright, talented, promising young girls and boys, women and men, get into the wrong relationships, friendships and peer groups. This results in all sorts of trouble being stirred up in their lives. So if you don't want drama to find its way inside your world, don't invite it in. Shut it out and be willing to remove yourself from the situation if necessary.

I also had to let go of someone very close to me when I was fifteen. He was my first boyfriend and I was head-over-heels for him, but I loved God more. Before the two of us parted ways, I had really committed my heart fully to Jesus Christ. I was living a saved lifestyle and had gotten actively involved in ministry at my church. I was getting really serious about pleasing the Lord! I had thrown myself into singing and finding out what God wanted to do with me.

Well, one day, I was driving to church and a friend began talking to me about him. "I thought you were with him and he was your boyfriend," she said, which totally confused me at first. I was totally unprepared for what I was about to hear. My friend, unfortunately, delivered the stunning news that my first love had been caught with another girl. The two of them were now an item and I was left out in the cold! I could hardly believe my ears and I felt like I was just going to die on the spot. It seemed like someone had reached into my chest, ripped my heart out and then punched me in the stomach.

Before that moment, I was confident that he and I had a good relationship even though he lived about two hours away from me. Yeah, I know. Long distance relationships are hard. We rarely got the chance to see each other but we talked all the time and he pretended to be *so* into me. Being that I was far away, there was no way I could have known he was being unfaithful. It's not like he was fessing up during our long phone conversations.

I was crushed into itty bitty pieces when I learned the reality of it all! When you think you're in love in your teens, news like that can really knock the wind out of your sails. Although it really isn't the end of the world, it can sure feel like it. I was *totally* devastated to the point where I had a hard time driving and concentrating. I cried and cried. I just could not understand how he could betray me like that.

There I was, thinking my boyfriend was loyal to me. He was in the church like me. We both were saved and seemed to share the same mindset. Everyone thought we were the perfect sweet little couple and were going to be together forever. We appeared to be doing great. Looking back on it, though, I should have seen it coming.

I was a virgin, but my boyfriend wanted to have sex. I didn't want to give my body away and wasn't willing to compromise. I didn't want to face the truth, but I was forced to see that he and I were not on the same page. I felt like I was being penalized for being good and saying no to premarital sex. My unwillingness to give up my virginity, however, cost me my boyfriend. But what I kept was far more valuable than what I lost.

When I confronted him about cheating on me, he made excuse after excuse. One of the "reasons" my ex gave me was he was having a hard time keeping up a long distance relationship. But I didn't want to hear that. When you're in a relationship that's honest and pure, distance shouldn't matter.

You're either going to be faithful or you're not, whether you live across the street from each other or across states. So, for me, that was a lame excuse. Humph!

Our happily ever after turned into happily *never* after. The Cinderella fairytale turned into a Jason horror film, so I broke things off. Even though it hurt something awful, I knew deep down that I had done the right thing by taking a stand for myself. I was an emotional mess, but I didn't go back to that guy. I stayed strong through the tears. I realized it was time to let go and I did.

Was it hard? Yes!

I didn't get over it overnight. It took me a while to really be free of the pain, but I survived. The more time passed, which felt like an eternity back then, it hurt less and less. And now that I am older and wiser, I realize that losing my ex-boyfriend was not really a loss at all. I was better off without him and deserved a person who wanted me for more than my body. If he couldn't see my value, he didn't deserve me. When I reflect on it today, I am glad I held my ground. He wasn't the right one for me anyway. If I had settled for him, I would not be with William, the best husband on the whole planet!

So I know breakups hurt. Losing friends is painful. Disconnecting from the peer groups you think you need to be relevant and popular, is not always the easiest thing in the world to do. But there comes a time in your life when you have to make bold, courageous decisions. Either you are going to do whatever it takes to run with the in-crowd, or you're going to be sold out to God and live your purpose.

SPARK**When you are faced with a choice, which will it be? Will you pursue fun and acceptance? Will you settle for second best because you don't feel you deserve better? Or will you be bold enough to stand out even if that means standing on your own? Will you stick up for yourself and defend what's right even when it's hard and uncomfortable? It is totally up to you.

There are more than enough opportunities to get caught up in the wrong thing in your school, community and even on the Internet. But you are the only one who can decide what you will and won't do. Personally, I was confronted with good and bad choices all the time in high school. I was no different from anyone else. I just made up my mind that I would be the girl with my head in the books and my heart and hands in the church. I studied hard and did well in school.

I could have hung out with the kids who were more interested in being cool and goofing off, but what would that have gotten me? I may have felt good temporarily, but I wanted more out of life. So I built my life around good people and activities. That's not to say I didn't make my mistakes, like getting expelled from school that one time. But I learned from my mess-ups. And when I realized something or someone wasn't quite right for me, I made the necessary changes. You have the power to do the same thing. Choose a positive path. Break off bad connections so you are only left with people who push you higher, not pull you lower.

Value Your Mentors

When you're young, trying to make good friendship choices can be tough. But there are other things you also need help with and advice about too, which is what makes mentors extra special. These are the trusted people God sends to teach, nurture, and get you moving in the right direction.

I have been blessed with so many great mentors in my life. They were just the coolest people! Like Pastor Tamara Bennett who I met after graduating from college at twenty one. When I moved from my home State of New Jersey all the way to California, the relocation was a big culture shock. I didn't know a single soul in the entire "Sunshine State" and felt like a fish out of water that had washed up on shore and would surely suffocate. It was a scary experience branching out on my own like that.

Before officially moving to Cali, I remember visiting her church with a friend. I felt an instant connection and believed, without a doubt, God had led me there. Somehow, I just knew it was where I was supposed to be. I had a really great feeling about it. So I asked, "Can I come to your church?"

I suppose it was a pretty odd request coming from a twenty one-year-old stranger. She replied, "You're going to move across the country and I don't even know you?" " Are you sure sister Melinda?" she said. But I was determined. And anyone who knows me will tell you, when I have my heart set on something, I do it.

This time was no different. I packed up, headed out and she welcomed me to the ministry. Though it may have seemed weird to others on the outside looking in, I'm so glad I listened to God. This woman became a true spiritual mother to me. She saw things in me I did not see in myself, pushed me into my purpose, trained me and helped me discover my true ministry. She was tough and focused. I admired that about her. She was also full of surprises and you would never know when you'd be put on the spot!

One day, without warning, she called me out on a Sunday and told me to lead worship that day. "What?" I thought to myself. I was absolutely terrified and trembling. I had never led praise and worship. Never, ever! Even though the woman I was living with at the time, Sister Natalie, had been a praise and worship leader for 10 years, I thought that was *her* calling, not mine. I was comfortable doing back up for sister Natalie. I was comfortable doing solos and maybe a sermonic solo. But out front? Me? No. Not me.

Once I was singled out for this unexpected assignment it sent fear all through me. I felt like hopping out of my seat, dashing down the center aisle, heading toward the nearest exit, leaving nothing but skid marks, and never looking back. But I didn't run away. Instead, I pushed through my fears. And you know what? That one experience changed my life, similar to the way my first Christmas solo in church had.

From the first time I ministered on the worship team, I knew my mentor had given me the right task. There was my spark! It was the one God had chosen for me. Worship was both my gift and my call. It was one of the most amazing revelations I ever received! But I may never have gotten it without submitting to a Godly teacher and advisor. To this very moment I honor and respect Pastor Bennett. She saw things in me that I never did and she pushed me to pursue them. Although she was tough, she was loving and she knew my potential spiritually. It is because of people like her, my god-mother Jackie and great friends that I found my spark! That I can walk boldly in what God has given me to do!

An excellent mentor will draw true greatness out of you! They will disciple you, improve you and help mature you. So value and treasure them. All throughout high school I had fantastic teachers who celebrated and encouraged me to be my best. Many of the lessons they taught me have stuck with me all these years.

**SPARK: Who are your advisors? Do you know? Who are the people who love you enough to tell you the truth and stop you from destroying your future? Is it your parents; grandparents; pastor; a community leader; guidance counselor; church mother; sister; brother; or a coach? Which people give you wise teaching to keep you out of trouble? Who has God placed in your path to help you make good decisions today that will impact the course of your future tomorrow? Think about it.

Once you identify them, be honest about your reaction to their advice. Are you listening to what they say? Is their instruction going in one ear and out the other? Are you rolling your eyes and talking back? Or are you really taking in what they say? Do you resent their advice when it isn't what you want to hear? Or do you realize they are simply telling you what is best for you and trying to help you?

Being teachable will lead to you receiving many benefits in your life. Any person who has been put on this earth to help craft you into a better person cannot do anything without your cooperation. If you're too stubborn and set in your ways to listen, you're going to miss out on some really good stuff.

If you reject your mentors, there is no way to be prepared for what God has for you. Proverbs 11:14 says, "Without wise leadership, a nation falls; there is safety in having many advisers." In other words, anyone who has no one to lead them or show them what to do will fall, and they will fail. Those who reach the highest heights are the ones willing to do what I talked about in chapter 2 and draw from the knowledge, and wisdom of others.

Are you willing? I hope so, because there is something extraordinary inside of you just waiting to shine for all to see. But it takes listening to God in order to find your spark and honoring the people He sends to influence you.

Learn From Others

During my years as a high school English teacher, I absolutely loved my job! Being a leader and positive role model for my students gave me life. When I looked into their eyes, I saw myself at that age. I remembered how the guidance of great teachers helped me find my way and I wanted to do the same thing for them.

So I developed a special program that allowed me to teach them things like social skills, etiquette and life skills in fun and creative ways. It was a life- changing experience for all of us, made possible by the great mentors I had growing up. How? Well, I believe that those mentored by greats become great mentors themselves. See how that works? Those who are taught well, become excellent teachers themselves.

Never stop learning from others. No one ever arrives at a place where they don't need to know anything else. If you want to make an impact and be a shining light for Christ, pay attention to the mentors all around you. Some will teach you what to do, others what *not* to do. There are even silent instructors whose actions help you learn, not their words. You may have to watch them from afar, but you can still gain a lot from paying attention.

After my music ministry first took off, it was a dream come true. But at the same time, I wasn't sure about a lot of things. There was so much to learn! I was brand new on the scene. Here I was, suddenly put under a bright spotlight after living for years with hardly anyone knowing who I was. That was a major adjustment! Before seeing my dreams come true, I felt like a really small person at the bottom of a gigantic mountain. I didn't know how to get from the bottom to the top. But then God lifted me up from the valley to the mountaintop by His power. Sometimes, it was scary up there despite all the good things about it like meeting the people I had always looked up to in gospel music. The biggest stars I grew up watching and admiring on television became a part of my life.

Still, there were tons of questions I needed answered like: *how do I do this? Where do I go for that? Who can I call for assistance with this aspect of my career?*

God, as He always does, sent people right to me to answer these questions. And I had *oodles* of them. Some of my mentors gave me bite-sized chunks of advice in passing. Others were more involved in molding and shaping my career. But no matter how big or small their lessons, they all made me a better person in some way. They prepared me to shine even brighter.

The same goes for you. The more you learn, the more you will be able to deliver powerful lessons of your own. Someday, you will be able to help a person reach *their* place of purpose. But you cannot skip over the process of being taught. The more teachable you are today, the more effective you will be later down the road.

Even though you are smart and capable of doing some things at the present moment, God knows when to release you into purpose. So be patient.

Don't get restless. Wait for your moment. Trust the people God has assigned to your life and treasure the relationships you have been given.

If you do, I promise it will pay off. You will look back on this very moment and be thankful you listened, and obeyed. When your date with destiny shows up, if you have heeded wise instruction and respected the leaders and teachers in your life, you will be ready to arise and shine for the glory of God.

Spark of Wisdom for Treasuring the People who Help you Shine:

In a similar way, you young people must submit to the elders. All of you must clothe yourselves with humility for the sake of each other, because: "God opposes the arrogant, but gives grace to the humble."

~1 Peter 5:5 (International Standard Version)

You must be taught before you can teach and be mentored before you can mentor. Remember that the greatest leaders are the most humble followers. Also, as you continue your pursuit of purpose, learn to separate good and bad relationships. The ones that are from God will stand the test of time and help you shine all the more brightly for Christ.

Shine Baby!

Position

Life gives you chances to
change your position and
pursue your dreams. Don't let
these moments pass you by!

Position

Did you see sixteen-year-old Gabby Douglas win the Olympic Gold Medal in gymnastics for the U.S. in August 2012? It was absolutely amazing! This young teen confidently got out there at the Olympic Games and made her dreams come true with plenty of hard work and perseverance. But did you know that before any of this ever happened Gabby and her mother Natalie had to make a great big sacrifice?

After five years of training at home in Virginia Beach, Virginia Gabby saw the 2008 Olympics where Shawn Johnson won the gold and silver medal for women's gymnastics. Right then, something clicked in this talented teenager's mind. She realized that if she wanted to be the best, she needed to be coached by the best—namely, Olympic medalist Shawn Johnson's coach, Liang Chow. The only problem was Mr. Chow lived thousands of miles away from Gabby in West Des Moines, Iowa. After discovering that distance problem, many of us would have woken ourselves up mid-dream and said, "This is impossible." But not Gabby!

After two years of pleading, once her mom Natalie finally agreed to let Gabby move in with a host family, The Partons, she packed up everything and took the leap. It was a *major* sacrifice for her to leave everything familiar to pursue a dream, and for her mother Natalie to actually let her go! These two were extraordinarily brave. As the saying goes, "Nothing ventured, nothing gained." They had their eyes focused on something greater, so they had to sacrifice greatly.

When Gabby changed her position, even though it was one of the hardest things she and her mom had to do, it opened up a whole new world of possibility. Sure, mom and daughter missed each other like crazy. Even though the Partons were loving and kind people, extended separation from your biological family is unimaginably difficult. So, understandably, Gabby got homesick sometimes. She even thought about quitting and returning to Virginia with her own family. But with the encouragement of her mom, Gabby stuck it out.

She continued being coached by Liang Chow, video chatting with her mother and preparing for her big shine baby moment. It all paid off too!

During the Olympics, Gabby wowed everybody with her energetic routines, strong physical conditioning, outstanding poise and remarkable control.

Because she was willing to change her position, she is now a sixteen-year-old Olympic champion who is the first woman of color ever to win an individual Olympic medal in gymnastics. Wow, right?

It is so inspiring to see Gabby living out her vision for her life and you can do it too. Just like her, I'm sure you have big dreams, cool ideas and colorful pictures in your mind of what life will be like someday. We all do, no matter how young or old. And it's a good thing you do. You *should* be looking forward to the future when your life's position—who, what, and where you are—will change. Even though you might not have to move thousands of miles away from home to do great things, your position in life will change in some way. How you think, who you hang around, what activities you participate in and the steps you take toward reaching your goals will determine how far you go in life.

By putting in the hard work to realize your ultimate potential and doing what you know is right, you will set yourself up for good things to come. A fantabulous future that beams more brightly than you can imagine awaits you. Deep down you know it. I know it. God definitely knows it even better than we do. He sees exactly what you are capable of becoming. You just need discipline and determination. When you have that, you can do anything you put your mind to… anything!

Take a risk so that you can ignite the spark within

The thing that separates dreamers from doers is a willingness to take calculated risks. That means, if you want to do more than just talk about being all you can be and actually start doing something about it, you have to take a chance. Go out on a limb. Test new waters. Know that you might fail, but try it anyway, because failure is not the end of the world. In fact, you learn your greatest life lessons from mistakes. So there is always a positive in every negative! Every day you can grow, improve and change for the better. But you have to spring into action first.

When life presented the opportunity for me to take a risk by changing my position and following my own dreams, I had a choice to make. I could have shied away from starting my own foundation for teen girls. I could have walked away from my chance to minister in song full time because it seemed crazy. But I opted for an alternate course. I said, "No matter how unrealistic and outrageous my goals seem, I'm going to jump at the chance... head first!" I took a big old leap of faith and because of that, I am now able to see that my dreams weren't crazy after all. They were given to me by God so I could do something with them.

I'm so glad I obeyed His voice telling me to step out in faith! That way, I don't have to come to the end of my life and wonder how different things would have been had I been braver. I need not ask, "Where would I be if I had just taken a chance to fail at something I loved?"

I don't want you to have to ask that either. Be determined to do everything you were put on earth to do. It's never too early or late to get started. From today onward I want you to live by a four-word quote: *"Live full. Die empty."* That means you should maximize your potential. Pour out everything you have inside you in an effort to make others' lives better. Use all your talents and capabilities to improve and impact the world around you for good. When you do that, your existence will be meaningful and joyful while you're giving inspiration, hope and help to others who need it.

Of course this will require lots of faith, especially when you have your sights set on very big things. Your common sense will scream out, "Have you lost your mind? You can't do that!" Come to think of it, that still happens to me a whole lot. But when the voices of doubt and worry get too loud, I stuff them down into my imaginary duffle bag, lock them away in the basement and keep moving ahead. If I don't, I'll shrink from risks and miss my moment to live my life the way God sees me doing it—fearless! He wants you to be fearless too.

Love your position

When my father Franklin was diagnosed with lung cancer, the odds of remission were not in his favor. He was 65 years old when the doctors told my mother he only had 6 months left to live. When I first heard the news, it tore me up inside. For a while, it didn't even seem real.

My dad, before he became very ill, had always been so strong. He held down multiple jobs, took care of his family, and seemed to carry the weight of the world with no strain. He was like my very own Superman, invincible.

Although I know no one does, at one point in life, it seemed like Franklin Pickett would live forever. But reality set in when I saw him at his most feeble. I sat at the bedside of my ailing father through his pain, making every single moment count, and figuring out funeral arrangements for the hero who made me believe I was a princess.

Those were dark days. The whole ordeal was devastating for our family. I remember one night, after flying home to visit my dad, I crawled into bed with him. I nuzzled my nose behind his ear and deeply inhaled, willing myself to remember the scent. It was a mix of *Versace Blue Jeans* cologne and *Dial* soap. I sat there so close to him and thought to myself, "If I died tomorrow, I'd want to die doing something I love." That thought came to me because my dad loved cooking and continued to do so until he couldn't anymore. He lived his dreams. He followed his passion.

Somehow, spending time with him during his final days made me reflective. My desire to live a purpose-driven life grew stronger. Sure, the situation was painful. No one wants to watch someone they love suffer. But God used it to help me reposition myself mentally.

I began examining my life from a different perspective and pondering whether I was really living and loving as I should. I began to see more clearly how short our time on earth is and why it is important to go after our destiny while we are here. I emerged from that difficult valley with a new outlook.

Now I say, cast off all fear, even if you have to walk through unfamiliar places. Once a fire is ignited in your heart to do something creative and exciting, don't ignore that burning! Let it drive you toward your divine purpose as I have done with music. My dad said two words to me almost everyday to push me forward. He said "Shine Baby!". He was pushing me to reach for the clouds of my purpose. His life and even death is my daily motivation.

Before officially entering the music industry, all I knew is that I loved to minister to others in song. I didn't realize the "industry world" was just that, a whole other world, complete with social hierarchies and secret handshakes.

Well, maybe not real handshakes, but it was definitely like a strange alternate universe that I didn't know much about! I wasn't aware of all the quirky rules that applied to successfully making it in the business.

I had to learn a lot of things on the fly, like how to assert myself, speak up for what I wanted, and challenge the powers that be, even though it was uncomfortable. My earlier giddiness was replaced with dread. There were a lot of days when I really wished I didn't have to deal with all the business stuff! Contracts, schedules, networking and learning to navigate my way through new relationships made my head spin. Why couldn't I just worship and build the lives of young women? I hadn't signed up for all the rest of it.

But the extra responsibility came with the territory. It was a necessary part of doing what I loved. Once I made a mental adjustment and fully embraced my role as both a businesswoman *and* singer, things began making sense. A little repositioning, sometimes physical, at other times mental, goes a long way.

Align Your Position And Your Priorities

As I finally settled into my role as a full-time recording artist, I began traveling and singing around the country, even the world, at the time. I had worked out most of my major jitters and nothing seemed impossible to me. I felt strong and capable, like I could balance my music career and domestic roles, and succeed at everything.

Ha! I couldn't have been more wrong.

Between hair and makeup appointments, sound checks and mini tour stops, I had hardly any time left. I was so exhausted from my "glamorous life" that after I kicked off the stilettos, I was too pooped to slide into the slippers and cook a decent meal. Something was terribly wrong with the pattern I had settled into. I knew I was too absorbed in my ministry pursuits. The raging storm on the ship of my life was caused by far too many commitments.

Something needed to go overboard.

Have you ever gotten too caught up with activities that your school work, relationships, and other areas of your life suffered? That's what was happening to me. I had lost my way. I had let my love for ministry and music over power my internal GPS designed to guide me, and tell me where to spend my time and energy. I was traveling two to three times per week. I couldn't keep up that pace. I needed to slow down, but I felt trapped.

What could I do? God had opened this door, right? Yes, but I was a wife and a mother first, before I was an artist. So I made a firm commitment to keep my priorities in order. It was time to pull off the lashes, put glamor girl away, ground the plane, unplug the stage microphone, and plug into my family.

I repented and asked God to give me the grace to be an incredible wife and mother. In return, I would give my heart for ministry to Him and trust the Lord to direct my steps. Soon after my shine baby moment led to a brief chaotic season, I stopped traveling during the week. I only accepted ministry engagements on weekends so I could take Lyric to school, tuck her in, cook dinner, and eat with the family. Finding your true spark requires discipline. You have to value your priorities and make time for them to be cultivated.

This transition was not easy. I disliked feeling that I was on the outside of all the cool happenings in the entertainment industry, but the slower pace rejuvenated me and made it much easier to serve my family and minister effectively. During quiet moments at home, I could hear the Holy Spirit speaking so clearly. I could sense in my heart that God was honoring my obedience to prioritize my family daily above the outside world.

Being on stage suddenly became far less important than listening to my daughter Lyric's song she wrote for her class performance. The rewards were different, but much greater because I was properly positioned in a posture of submission to God's will.

You have to take a step back sometimes and make sure you are focusing on the things that matter most. Otherwise, your schedule will get cluttered and the things you should be pouring energy into will be neglected. Don't let that happen to you. Get your priorities together and you will be able to shine more brightly.

Spark of Wisdom for Positioning Yourself to Shine for Christ:

Humble yourselves, therefore, under God's mighty hand, that he may lift you up in due time.

The most important position you will ever assume is down on your knees in prayer and supplication, seeking God's will for your life. He knows the path you need to take, so don't get consumed with activities and forget to pray. In the Kingdom of God, the way up is down. When you humble yourself before God, He will do the exalting.

~1 Peter 5:6 (New International Version)

Shine Baby!

Problems

We all have issues, struggles and obstacles that stand between us and our destiny. God doesn't remove them. He just teaches us to master them.

Problems

Problems. *Ugh!* Who needs 'em... or wants 'em for that matter? Nobody I know of desires to deal with issues. I sure don't! But somehow we all have a few troubles that seem to follow us around, kind of like an unwanted stray cat searching for food, you know? At every turn, those bothersome burdens linger in the shadows, waiting for us to *give* in so they can *get* in.

It's a good thing being problem-free isn't one of the requirements we have to meet in order to shine and be on fire for God. If it were, I would be *so* disqualified, like really. So would you. In fact, there would be absolutely nobody out of the 7 billion people on earth that God could choose to do His awesome work for Him. Thinking about it that way, aren't you glad God can still use us to shine brightly even with our hang-ups and issues? You can ignite your world with that spark that God has given you regardless of the problems that you may face.

Now, of course that doesn't mean we don't have to work hard to defeat our problems. We can't just lie down in the middle of the road and let life's challenges run us over like a big old bus. Even though our personal struggles may get the best of us from time to time, God expects us to put up a mean fight and continue to grow. Just like everyone else, I'm on a mission to constantly improve.

Don't Let Problems Hold You Back

My ongoing battle, one of my biggest problems, has been with fear since my younger days. It became a huge obstacle during my senior year in High

School as I continued to bury my head in the books and bust my brain to make good grades, just as I always had. But I studied *especially* hard in my final year, even while holding down a 30-hour-a-week job at an insurance company. On top of that, I was heading up the dance team at church, mentoring other girls and staying very active in the community.

And all the while, I was nursing a dream to go to Washington, DC to attend the one and only Howard University. To this day it's one of the best historically black college universities (HBCU's) in the nation and I had my heart completely set on making it there. Every day, I could see it, taste it, smell it and breathe it. I was on my way!

What really inspired me to pursue this goal was seeing two of my biggest role models (Nicole and Regina) go to HBCU's. Everything in me wanted to join in that proud heritage right along with them. And from the looks of things, one of my greatest dreams was about to become a reality. I got accepted into Howard University! It was almost unreal to realize that, finally, this Jersey girl's work had paid off. I was on my way to DC, the Capital of America. I thought, "Wow, this is actually happening." It tripped me out.

When I received my set of keys for my on-campus dorm room, everything was all set and ready. But *I* wasn't. You remember the problem called "fear" lingering in the shadows that I talked about at the start of this chapter? Well, it wrapped itself around my neck, held me in a choke hold and wouldn't let go. Sadly, I let it suffocate my confidence, paralyze and stop me dead in my tracks. So I didn't end up going to Howard.

I was too terrified to go, so I rejected my golden keys of opportunity. Now I understand full well what our 32nd president, Franklin Delano Roosevelt meant when he said his now infamous quote:

"Only thing we have to fear is fear itself." Fear is a sneaky little liar that whispers false things in your ear and robs you of the courage to step out and move forward.

Fear tricked me. It told me not to branch out and do what was really in my heart because I would *definitely* fall flat on my face. I would *never* live up to my parents' high expectations of me. My grades would tank and I'd end up disappointing the two people in the world that believed in me more than anyone else.

Fear said "You're a fraud Melinda and you're not smart enough for Howard." And just like a hungry fish that swallows the fisherman's *hook*, gets reeled in with the fishing line, and ends up weighed down in the water by the sinker, I took the bait. I bought into the deception, "hook, line, and sinker."

I agreed with fear and let it lead me right to my community college where I enrolled for a semester. But thank God I snapped out of my fear-filled daze quickly! A single term was all the time it took for this girl to get herself together. Although I never did attend Howard University, I transferred to Rutgers University—a really great college right in my home state. So it all worked out in the end and I learned a very valuable lesson that I want to pass along to you.

If you don't whip your problems and get them in check, they'll whip and defeat you. Yours might not be paralyzing fear. But we all have *at least* one hurdle in our lives that seems too high to get over. It could be low self-esteem, shyness, anxiety, or even some sort of bad habit (or several!) we need to break.

Whatever your personal struggle is, get it *out* of your way so it won't *stand* in your way. Pray about the obstacle. Trust God to help you overcome it and not be controlled by it. I know that is *much* easier said than done, but it's possible. You may have some falls and setbacks, but hey, don't we all? Each of us struggles sometimes with problems. But my point is you don't have to let them defeat you or rob you of your moment to shine for God. You can conquer anything with the help of the Lord, lots of persistence, patience with yourself and determination.

Get Over Your People Problem

Children crack me up with the hilarious things they do, but I also think it's pretty neat how free and comfortable they are with being themselves. Young kids make funny faces; do silly dances; put on crazy outfits; make up goofy songs; fall down in public; tell corny jokes; and act as loopy as they want, without ever worrying about what anyone around them thinks. I just *love* that! My baby girl Honour-Smile is all smiles day in and day out! Just like her name, she finds something to laugh about everyday.

But as they get older, something happens to them that we all experience. The once carefree little ones become more self-conscious older ones. They learn what is "acceptable" or "unacceptable" based on societal norms and the opinions of others.

Remember when I told you at the beginning of the book how I started feeling like I didn't fit in once I became a teenager? Well, in some ways, we all become more aware of our surroundings as we grow up.

We look for people we can identify with, which is completely normal. But when people's attitudes toward us, thoughts and ideas about us, and perceptions of us begin taking over our lives and making us neurotic about changing our very essence, that's when it gets problematic. Even though we are discovering our inner spark of uniqueness within us, there are times when people can cause us to doubt and fear.

If we start wondering if our hair, clothes and other features are good enough by others' standards, we have crossed the line over into the "people problem" area. This is where we look for approval, applause and adoration from members of society before we feel worthy. This is a big no-no, because you can't please everyone. If you measure your worth by how others treat you and what they say about you, oh boy!

That can lead to all sorts of stuff: low self-esteem, depression, eating disorders and even going along with the crowd (when you *know* it's wrong) just to fit in. I suffered from low self-esteem, insecurity and fear of others. What I thought was meant for bad, God used those frail traits to use me for His glory. It's ok to admit where you're lacking as long as you know where to go for healing!

So if you want to be a trailblazer, you have to get comfortable with being honest about yourself and with being different. That means there's not much room for insecurity. You know why? Because when you look around, there won't be anything or anyone out there that embodies the *exact* vision you see. You will have to believe in your dreams, your goals and yourself in order to go after your destiny. You have a spark. One that can ignite the world. You are unique. God doesn't want you to be a carbon copy. You were made to blaze a trail, not follow in someone else's footsteps.

Think about how the creative team at Apple must have felt when they came up with iPhone. It was totally different and nothing could be compared to it. Development of what was to become the iPhone began back in 2004 with about 1000 workers. It was highly confidential and was called "Project Purple."

Just imagine the process. Everyone involved in the development of this new gadget that would take the world by storm had to be confident that their ideas would work. They had to have faith in their belief that this was something special. Good thing they did. Nowadays, iPhone is one of the top-selling phones in the world and millions of people own one, including me. Who knew these workers would cook up something so successful and awesome? They dared to be different and take a risk, and it paid off big time!

When it comes to music, I like to be different too. But everyone doesn't always agree with me or support my choices. Once there was this song I loved that was written by a relatively unknown worship artist from Greece. I heard the melody and immediately, it connected with me. I knew within myself it was something I wanted to sing. I believed it would really bless other people who heard it even though it didn't have the typical traditional gospel sound.

I was so excited. I went to a friend at the time and said, "Oh my Gosh! Listen to this song. Isn't this powerful?"

"Yes!" they responded. "But I hope *you're* not going to try and sing it though. People won't relate to this kind of music. It won't work."

I was so annoyed and crushed. It felt like déjà vu! In chapter one I told you how, when I was thirteen, a trusted mentor told me, "You'll never make it in music because you aren't black enough and your voice doesn't squall enough." Here again, someone close to me was telling me what I couldn't or shouldn't do based on their idea of what was right for me.

Too bad I let my *people problem* get the best of me. I was so concerned with this person's approval that I immediately closed myself in and never wanted to sing the song. Because of fear and insecurity, I allowed an outside opinion to have a negative impact on me and change what I truly believed in my heart was God-sent.

That's how we are sometimes. We'll know what God is saying. But then, we'll allow the voices of others to shift our focus and make us too afraid to do what was originally instructed. And you know what's so crazy? This same song is now being sung across the nation, by people of all races and ethnicities. It is reaching, touching and blessing so many lives as I *knew* it would. I guess I wasn't out of my mind after all, huh?

No Problem Is Too Hard for God

I was the baby girl and my family really kept me busy with church. I had just enough time to do homework, chores and Bible study. I didn't really stretch myself with too much as a kid and young teen. I had the opportunity to express myself in the church choir, as a part of the step team, as well as through mime. But outside of the ministry of creative arts and music, I was too scared to try anything else.

Clearly, as I've said before, that nagging fear issue has been with me most of my life. But as I have grown in my faith in God, I see all the ways I have developed and matured in this area. By His grace, I have been able to conquer so many obstacles and overcome setbacks I never dreamed I could. Looking back over my life, I can see the hand of God at work, helping me through my issues. He's still working. I not only found my spark in worship and in music, but I also found it in my organization for teen girls. I found my spark in designing weddings and events. I ignitied my world through writing books, speaking at inspirational events and creating resources for others. Yes, I had fear but more than that I had a crazy faith that went to work for me!

One big lesson was driven home for me after having my baby girl, Lyric. Even before she was born, my husband and I were super excited! We knew that having a daughter would give us the chance (especially me!) to dress her up in really cute clothes and take pictures to show off how beautiful she was to everyone. I still love doing that. I'm such a proud mom! So anyway, when our brown beauty made her arrival, we were ecstatic. My first thought was to go to the mall and get her a special outfit for her pictures. So I purchased a beautiful pink gown made of silk and chiffon.

On Lyric's very first day home, I carefully dressed her. I made sure all the tulle was just right so it would be nice and poofy just like a Cinderella gown. I was pleased as punch as I stood back and looked at my princess lying there. Everything was perfect I thought, until my hubby William entered the room with a sad look on his face. He said, "We purchased everything but her tiara. *Every* princess needs a tiara!" At first I was bummed that I forgot the once piece we needed to complete Lyric's ensemble. But then it hit me! She *did* have a sparkly tiara. But it was the "invisible" kind that she would never have to take off. It was her beautiful spirit that shined more brightly than a bejeweled headpiece.

So right at that moment, William and I both prayed for our baby girl that her "tiara" would be made of precious and strong jewels of wisdom, love, and the light of Christ that would never fade. "Guide her through life each and every day," we asked the Lord. "Let her life please You." After William and I prayed over our new bundle together, we both realized the physical doesn't matter nearly as much as the spiritual.

And when it comes to problems that present themselves in *your* life, the same thing is true. What's going on inside far outweighs what's going on outside. That's why God is concerned with the inner you, which is the real you. He's not after the dolled up, public person that can pretend to be someone else. He knows your authentic self, with all your struggles that are often invisible to the world. He's also more than able to help you overcome any problem. No matter how complex it seems, remember that nothing is too hard for God.

Problems cannot be avoided. We all have them. But we don't have to allow them to control us. Daily, pray that God will help you identify your issues, submit them to Him, and soar above them. Even when you feel overwhelmed, remember that there is no obstacle that can stop you unless you allow it to. When you give your worries, cares and struggles to God, they won't get the best of you and they won't dim your light.

Every time fear makes things seem impossible, God reminds me that I can do all things through Him. When I get caught up wondering what others are thinking, what they will say and if they will accept me or not, God lets me know He accepts me. He thinks I am a gem and loves me just the way I am. Whenever I feel drained and exhausted from worrying about problems, God tells me to rest and trust in Him, and let Him take care of me.

He is saying the same thing to you today, which is why it's no mistake or coincidence that you're reading this book. You have a spark within you. Seek God on where to find it! Ask Holy Spirit on how to ignite it. It's there. When you begin to follow God's plan for you that's when you will find it! It's what makes you unique and special.

God knows all of your inward parts, so He knew from the beginning what problems would come along to hinder you in your quest to shine for Him. That's why your loving Heavenly Father is always working to make sure you are whole from the inside out. It's not the exterior that matters most, but the interior that determines whether we can live up to God's great big plans for us! So take the faith and find your spark. You will ignite the world!

Shine Baby!

"Ah, Sovereign LORD, you have made the heavens and the earth by your great power and outstretched arm. Nothing is too hard for you."
Jeremiah 32:27 (New International Version)